CHARLES DICKENS

The Man Who Had Great Expectations

DIANE STANLEY

&

PETER VENNEMA

illustrated by

DIANE STANLEY

Morrow Junior Books
NEW YORK

The authors wish to thank Bert G. Hornback, Professor of English at Bellarmine College
in Louisville, Kentucky, for his incisive reading of this text.

Gouache was used for the full-color artwork. The text type is 15-point Weiss Roman.

Printed in Singapore at Tien Wah Press.

1   2   3   4   5   6   7   8   9   10

Library of Congress Cataloging-in-Publication Data • Stanley, Diane. Charles Dickens / Diane Stanley and Peter Vennema ; illustrated by Diane Stanley.   p.   cm.
Summary: Follows the life and writing career of the popular nineteenth-century English novelist.   ISBN 0-688-09110-5.—ISBN 0-688-09111-3 (lib. bdg.)   1. Dickens,
Charles, 1812–1870—Biography—Juvenile literature.   2. Novelists, English—19th century—Biography—Juvenile literature.   [1. Dickens, Charles, 1812–1870.
2. Authors, English.]   I. Vennema, Peter.   II. Title.   PR4581.S628   1993
823′.8—dc20   91-41552   CIP   AC

For John,
who walked
with us
in the footsteps
of Dickens
and was a
good sport
about it

*A*ll his life Charles Dickens would remember a particular day when he was nine years old, and something his father said. They were out walking together and had stopped, as they often did, to admire a handsome rose-brick house called Gad's Hill Place. With its lovely bay windows and sweeping lawn, it seemed as grand as a palace to them.

Then John Dickens told his son that if he worked very hard, someday he might live in that house. The thought took Charles's breath away. The sort of person who would live in Gad's Hill Place would be a distinguished man of taste and education. His father believed that *Charles* could someday be like that. All he had to do was work hard.

He could not have known on that day how far he would fall and how high he would rise, and that he really would live in that house, and that he would die there.

When Charles looked back on his childhood, these were the happy years. They lived in a snug brick row house in Chatham, east of London. It had a little garden and, across the road, there was a meadow where the children could play. He was in the care of his beloved nursemaid, Mary Weller, who comforted his childish sorrows. She also terrified him with blood-curdling horror stories that he adored, though they gave him nightmares. He spent wonderful hours in his little attic room reading from his father's set of novels. He went for days imagining himself to be one of his storybook heroes—Robinson Crusoe, Roderick Random, or Peregrine Pickle.

He and his older sister Fanny went to a day school run by a scholar named William Giles, who recognized Charles's intelligence and imagination and gave him special attention. He had a group of school friends who all wore white beaver hats and called themselves Giles's Cats. Together they played carefree, boisterous games and explored Chatham and nearby Rochester with its grand cathedral and ruined castle. They went rowing in the summer and skating in the winter.

But when Charles was ten, his father was transferred to London, and his happy childhood came to a sudden end.

John Dickens had many wonderful qualities. He worked hard at his job in the Navy Pay Office and was loving to his wife, Elizabeth, and to his children. He had many friends and loved to invite them to the house in the evening for a bowl of steaming punch and lively conversation. But he had one terrible fault: He spent more money than he made.

In the ten years of Charles's life, the family had lived in six different houses, each poorer than the one before. And as the number of mouths to feed kept growing (there were eight children in all), the family fell deeper and deeper into debt.

When they reached London, Charles was shocked to learn that he would not be sent to school—they couldn't afford it. Fanny was able to go to the Royal Academy of Music because she had won a scholarship there as a boarding student. But Charles merely stayed at home and made himself useful by cleaning his father's boots and minding the younger children. His parents seemed to have forgotten him and all his ambitions.

As their money problems worsened, Elizabeth decided to help by opening a school. So they moved again, this time to a house large and respectable enough for "Mrs. Dickens's Establishment." It was far grander than they could afford, and since not one student ever came to the school, their situation grew even worse. Charles remembered later that "we got on very badly with the butcher and the baker and that very often we had not too much for dinner."

To pay the butcher or baker, the Dickens family was forced to sell things. Charles would be sent to the pawnshop from time to time with an armload of books. It made him sad to part with them, for reading was now his only escape from drudgery. But the books were soon followed out of the house by teaspoons, chairs, pictures, and carpets. Charles felt humiliated, lonely, and neglected. And it got worse.

Two days after his twelfth birthday, Charles Dickens was sent to work at Warren's blacking factory. From eight in the morning till eight at night, he worked in a dark room, covering pots of blacking—or boot polish—and pasting on labels. Other children worked there, too, but they were not like his old friends. They were poor boys with rough manners who referred to him scornfully as the "young gentleman."

Worse still, two weeks later his father was arrested for debt and sent to the Marshalsea Prison, where he had to stay until his debts were paid. Elizabeth and the children were allowed to join him there, the whole family living in one room—everyone, that is, except Charles. The blacking factory was too far from the prison for him to get back before the gates were shut at night. So he lived in a cheap boarding house. From Monday morning until Saturday night he was on his own with "no advice, no counsel, no encouragement, no consolation, no support from anyone."

At night he wandered through the dark city. His clothes were shabby. He had no friends. Instead of growing into a fine gentleman, he had descended to the streets.

The memory of that time was so painful that, even as a grown man, Charles could not walk through those streets without the sting of tears coming to his eyes. And years later, when he became a writer, his stories were filled with orphaned and abandoned children, debtors' prisons, workhouses, and the grim and degrading lives of the poor.

John Dickens was released from prison after a little over three months. His mother had died, leaving him more than enough money to pay his debts.

But for Charles, the nightmare went on. His father seemed content to keep him at the blacking factory. It happened that his employer moved Charles and another boy near a window, where the light was better. The sight of these two children working so nimbly at their tasks was amusing, and a crowd often gathered to watch. John Dickens soon heard about it and became angry. It made him ashamed for his son to be on display like that. He took Charles out of the warehouse and sent him back to school.

Wellington House Academy wasn't a very good school. The headmaster was cruel and often beat the children with a ruler. But Charles was overjoyed to be in *any* school, among healthy and high-spirited boys who had time for games.

They even kept pet mice in the schoolroom, including one especially well-trained fellow who lived inside a Latin dictionary. He "ran up ladders, drew Roman Chariots, shouldered muskets," and even appeared in little plays in a toy theater. "He might have achieved great things," Dickens recalled, "but for having the misfortune to make his way in a triumphant procession to the capitol, when he fell into a deep inkstand and was dyed black and drowned."

When he was fifteen, Charles ended his education for good. His first job was as an office boy for an attorney, but he found it dull. So he taught himself to write shorthand. This was very hard and took him months to learn, but he soon got work as a court reporter and, later, as a journalist who reported on government. What he saw in those days did not make him think very highly of lawyers or politicians. He called them a "mob of brainless windbags."

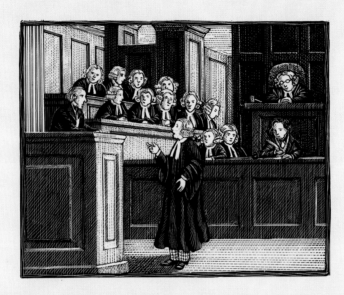

It was during this time that he met a pretty banker's daughter named Maria Beadnell. He was well aware that he was not the sort of suitor the prosperous Beadnells wanted for their daughter, but once Charles got hold of an idea, it was almost impossible for him to put it down. He was possessed with the idea that he worshipped and adored Maria Beadnell. For four years he wrote her endless letters and poems. He bought four new waistcoats and a silk neckerchief and took to wearing kid gloves. He squeezed his feet into fashionable boots with pointed toes and almost crippled himself walking across town at night, just to look up at the window of the room where she slept. He fussed over her spoiled little dog and tried very hard to dazzle her parents with his wit.

Mr. Beadnell, however, was suspicious of this persistent young man and soon discovered his shameful past. Suddenly Maria was whisked off to Paris to "finish her education." When she returned, she was cold and capricious. The message was unmistakable: He was not good enough for her.

Charles was heartbroken and his pride was deeply hurt. For years he would think with bitter longing of the beautiful Maria Beadnell. He could not guess that one day they were to meet again. So he poured his restless energy into long daily walks, often ranging as far as twenty miles through busy streets or country lanes, and his spirits began to lift. As he walked, he looked into shop windows and down dark alleys, absorbing the sounds and smells around him. He watched the people he passed—the rich "swells" in their tight jackets and beaver hats, refined ladies who rode in carriages, shopgirls and rowdy drunks, pickpockets and fishmongers, and ragged children who slept in doorways. He began to make up stories about these people and then to write them down.

One evening, "with fear and trembling," he dropped one of his stories into a "dark letter box in a dark office up a dark court in Fleet Street." It was the office of the *Monthly Magazine*, which often published the work of beginning writers, though it didn't pay anything. Charles waited nervously for the next issue to come out, then searched its pages hopefully for "A Dinner at Poplar Walk." And there it was, "in all the glory of print!" His "eyes so dimmed with pride and joy," he recalled, "they could not bear the street." He had to go somewhere private for half an hour to compose himself.

He wrote many more stories for the *Monthly Magazine*, under the pen name Boz. This was a family baby name he had borrowed from his little brother. People began to remark that whoever this Boz was, he was a very funny writer. His stories were so popular that they were published as a book called *Sketches by Boz*. He was now officially an author.

Charles could now afford to marry, and the lady he chose was Catherine Hogarth, the pretty, sleepy-eyed daughter of a newspaper editor.

Charles was not wildly in love, as he had been with Maria Beadnell. Perhaps he just felt that a successful man should have a wife. Whatever his reason, it was one of the worst mistakes he ever made. Looking back on his marriage years later, he was convinced that Catherine "would have been a thousand times happier if she had married another kind of man." He would have been happier, too.

Whereas Charles was brilliant, orderly, and high-spirited, Catherine was an ordinary woman, incompetent in household affairs, who was worn down over the years by bearing their ten children. Her sisters, first Mary and later Georgina, lived with them and did the things Catherine couldn't manage. Charles often had to order the food, keep the books, and make arrangements for the house. "It would have been better," he later wrote, "if my wife had helped me more."

Divorce was out of the question; it was considered scandalous in those days. In the end, after living together for twenty-two years, Charles and Catherine separated. Though still married, they lived apart for the rest of their lives.

Shortly before his marriage, a publisher had come to Dickens to propose a new project. Would he be willing to write some amusing paragraphs to go with a book of illustrations by the well-known artist Robert Seymour? The book would come out in monthly installments. It would be about a club of sportsmen who go hunting and fishing and are forever falling out of boats or barely missing one another with their guns.

This gave Charles an even better idea. Instead of a series of clever paragraphs, he would write a book himself, and Robert Seymour would illustrate *it*. There would be a club, and the characters might do a little hunting, but mostly they would travel about and have adventures. And so *The Posthumous Papers of the Pickwick Club* (or, more commonly, *The Pickwick Papers*) was begun.

Then, tragically, Seymour died. Another illustrator, Hablôt Knight Browne, known as Phiz, took over the illustration of each installment. It was a perfect match.

Dickens began to relax a bit and have fun with the Pickwickians. He gave up the club idea, which hadn't been his anyway. Instead of a string of disconnected episodes, the story began to have more of a plot. And it became decidedly funny. Wonderful new characters began popping into his head, and he described them with rich and unexpected detail. It was so fresh and original and full of glorious nonsense that all over England people began reading *Pickwick* and laughing uproariously.

The Pickwick Papers became a national mania. People began selling Pickwick hats, Pickwick canes, coats, cigars, and jokebooks. A gentleman returning from Egypt reported seeing "Pickwick" carved on one of the pyramids. And Charles Dickens had become, at the age of twenty-five, world famous.

Mary Hogarth

Charles and Catherine had a son they named Charles, Jr., and they soon moved to a bigger house. They were joined by Catherine's seventeen-year-old sister, Mary. While Charles was quick to find fault with his wife, he idolized Mary. "So perfect a creature never breathed," he said. To him she was a "winning, happy, amiable companion, sympathizing with all my thoughts and feelings more than anyone...ever did, or will." It must have seemed obvious to everyone that Charles had married the wrong sister.

One evening, shortly after she came to live with them, Mary suffered a sudden heart attack. The following afternoon, she died in Charles's arms. Overcome with grief, he took a ring from her finger and kept it until his death. He was too miserable to write, and for the only time in his life, he failed to meet his deadlines. "I don't think there ever was love like that I bear her," he wrote.

He never forgot Mary. Because she died so young—never to grow old, never to disappoint him—she became his image of womanly perfection. She lived on in his books as the angelic Agnes of *David Copperfield,* the devoted Lucy Manette in *A Tale of Two Cities,* and, of course, the tragic Little Nell of *The Old Curiosity Shop.* Readers often find these characters too good to be believable. But they were real to Dickens—they were all Mary.

When he returned to his writing, Dickens worked at a frenzied pace, finishing *Pickwick* and beginning a new novel at the same time. *Oliver Twist* was set far from the jolly, respectable world of *The Pickwick Papers*. In the "cold, wet, shelterless midnight streets" of the crime-ridden London slums, children were starved and beaten. They were lowered down chimneys to sweep them out or put to work in unheated factories for fourteen hours a day. Some took to the streets to become thieves, and some died there.

Oliver Twist is not just a story about an orphan boy who runs away to London and falls in with bad friends. It is also about the suffering of the English people after the Industrial Revolution, when huge masses of workers were forced off farms and into factories, mills, and mines. Everyone had to work just to survive. Even children as young as five worked until late at night at monotonous and dangerous tasks. Yet still they might not have enough to eat. And even if they did, many died in terrible accidents in the factories and mines. Diseases such as tuberculosis and cholera killed still more. Anyone desperate enough to steal a loaf of bread could get hung for it.

For the rest of his life, Charles Dickens described this pitiless world in rich detail. In book after book he painted such horrifying pictures of the despairing poor that this period in history is often called Dickensian England. He became the mirror in which England was reflected. And the people were shocked and moved by what they saw. They began to pass reform laws, to build better houses and even schools for the poor. No matter how successful Dickens became, he never forgot the ragged child he had once been, and he never stopped working to ease the suffering of the poor.

Much of the power of Dickens's writing comes from the almost endless parade of memorable characters he put into every novel. He brought them so wonderfully to life because he imagined them so clearly. His son, Charley, remembered that "I have often and often heard him complain that he could not get the people of his imagination to do what he wanted, and that they would insist on working out their histories in *their* way, and not his. I can very well remember his describing them flocking round the table in the quiet hours…each one of them claiming and demanding instant personal attention."

Some of Dickens's greatest characters were villains, as unique as they were dreadful—from the crafty Fagin of *Oliver Twist* and the oily Uriah Heep of *David Copperfield* to the miserly Ebineezer Scrooge of *A Christmas Carol*. Others were pathetic, such as mad old Miss Havisham in *Great Expectations*. And, comic genius that he was, Dickens gave us many of the funniest characters in literature. Not the least of these is Mr. Micawber of *David Copperfield,* who is always in debt but ever hopeful that something will "turn up." This lovable but clownish character, with his pompous speech, was a portrait of Dickens's own father.

These characters sometimes came to be as real to the reading public as they were for their creator. Such was the case with Little Nell. People all over the world read the newest chapter of *The Old Curiosity Shop* every month, eager to learn what would become of Nell and her poor, demented grandfather. Was the innocent child doomed to die?

In America, the suspense was so great that New Yorkers waited at the pier for the boat from England carrying the latest installment. They shouted anxiously to the passengers aboard the ship as it came into harbor, "Is Little Nell dead?"

She was, and the whole world mourned. In England, one member of Parliament was said to have read the death scene while riding in a train. Bursting into tears, he cried, "He should not have killed her!" and threw it out the window!

Dickens was very popular in America, and he was often invited to visit there. When he was thirty years old, he decided to make the trip, with the idea of writing a book about it when he returned. He expected the book to be full of praise for a democratic country where all men were equal and everyone had a chance to succeed.

On January 4, 1842, he and Catherine set sail for the new world. It was a stormy passage. As the ship rolled, passengers were flung about in their cabins. Everyone was seasick. The waves struck the deck with such force that they crushed the lifeboats. The smokestack had to be tied down to keep it from falling over and setting the ship on fire.

At last they arrived in Boston. Even before the ship docked, reporters came aboard to interview Dickens. He should have known then what lay ahead.

Everywhere he went, he was mobbed by fans, who begged for locks of his hair and tore off bits of his clothing as keepsakes. He had to hire a secretary to handle all the mail. Sculptors and painters insisted on doing his portrait. And all America wanted autographs. He was stared at and talked about as if he were some curiosity.

In spite of all the frenzy, he liked Boston. He thought it was a clean and pretty place, full of refined people. The great writers and intellectuals of the day entertained him, and some of them became his lifelong friends.

But as he went farther south, he became more critical. He was shocked by the disgusting habit of chewing tobacco and spitting. Americans did it on the street, in hotels, and in railway carriages. But he could not believe his eyes when he sat in a White House waiting room before meeting with the President and watched elegant gentlemen spit on the carpet!

And then there were the newspapers, which were praising him one minute and attacking him the next. In one of his speeches, Dickens had complained that American publishers felt free to print and sell his books without asking his permission or paying him a penny. The American press responded to this reasonable complaint with outrage. Doggedly Dickens repeated his opinion everywhere he traveled, and every time he was viciously criticized for it.

But most of all, he was horrified by the hideous institution of slavery. "They say the slaves are fond of their masters," Dickens later wrote in his book *American Notes.* "That, of course, was why the newspapers were full of advertisements for runaway slaves. That was why nine out of ten of these ads described the runaways as chained, manacled, mutilated, maimed, or branded."

After six grueling months, Dickens was fed up with Americans, who seemed to talk of nothing but money and politics. He was convinced that nowhere in the world were there "so many intensified bores as in these United States." "This is not the republic I came to see" was his disappointed conclusion. "This is not the republic of my imagination." He was ready to go home.

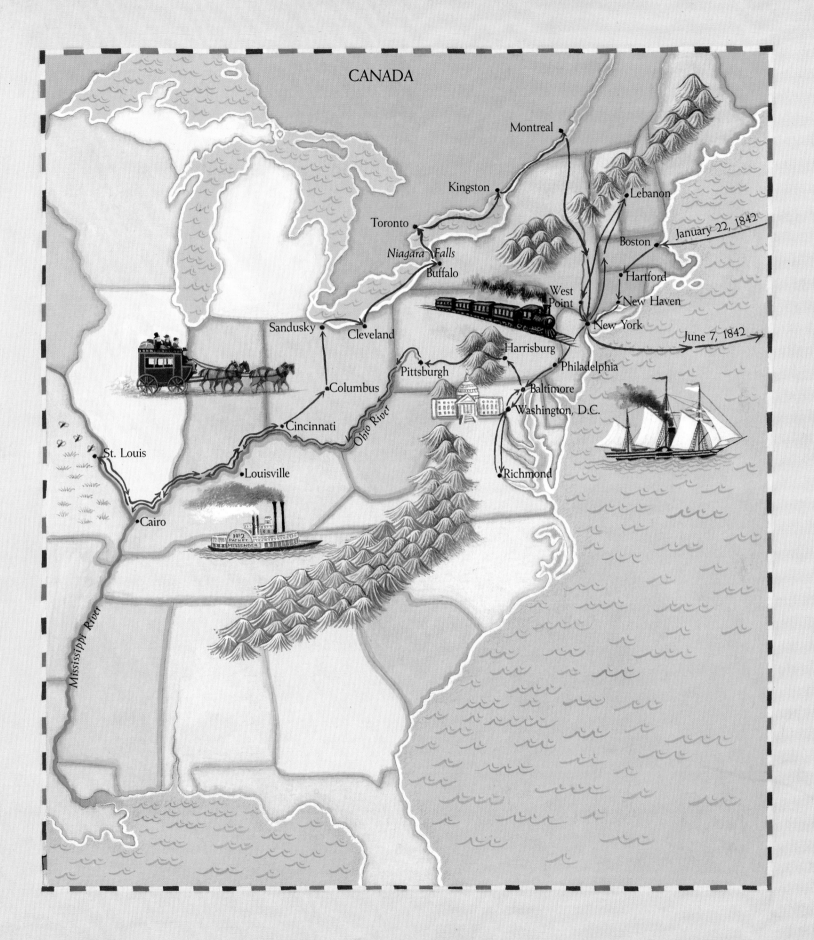

CANADA

Montreal

Kingston

Toronto

Niagara Falls

Buffalo

Sandusky

Cleveland

Lebanon

Boston   January 22, 1842

West
Point

Hartford

New Haven

New York

June 7, 1842

Columbus

Pittsburgh

Harrisburg

Philadelphia

Cincinnati

Ohio River

Baltimore

Washington, D.C.

St. Louis

Louisville

Richmond

Cairo

N°2
PACKET
MESSENGER

Mississippi River

Back in England, Dickens began work on *American Notes*. But writing was a lonely occupation, and he was a most outgoing man. So when Dickens put down his pen, he loved to gather his many friends together for parties and amateur theatricals. His plays were serious undertakings. There were elaborate sets, costumes, and props. In fact, they were so well done that Dickens sometimes put them on for the public to raise money for charity. He even performed for Queen Victoria.

His parties were joyous affairs with music and dancing, guessing games, and blindman's buff. Dickens often entertained his guests with comic songs and magic tricks. He could turn a box of bran into a guinea pig and after that, set a fire blazing in a top hat (which would be undamaged), put an empty saucepan over it, and magically produce a plum pudding.

Dickens often called himself the Sparkler, and he never sparkled so brightly as at Christmas. And so it was natural that he would want to celebrate the Christmas spirit in his writing. In the fall of 1843, he began work on the first of five books he would write to be published at Christmas. He worked on it with loving care, doing much more rewriting than usual. As he wrote, he "wept and laughed and wept again." And so, it turned out, did his readers, who bought *A Christmas Carol* by the thousands. Even today his little book is a part of Christmas all over the world, and it is, without a doubt, the best known and most beloved of Dickens's works.

The years passed and each new book added to his fame and prosperity. He looked like an important man, too—wearing fashionable whiskers and extravagant clothes.

Every day brought piles of mail from all over the world, written by adoring fans. One evening he spotted a letter written in a familiar handwriting. His heart pounded wildly as he recognized it as that of Maria Beadnell! She wrote that she was married now and had two daughters. But she had read all his books and she wanted to see him. Charles couldn't get over it. The thought of meeting her again after all those years, to have *her* seek *him* out, for him to appear before her not as a struggling suitor but as a great man—well, dreams did come true sometimes!

At last the day for the meeting arrived. When he saw her, he was stunned. The woman who stood before him was middle-aged and undeniably fat. But that, as he later wrote, "was not much." After all, he was older, too. But when she began to giggle and toss her curls childishly about, to flutter her eyelashes and give him meaningful glances from behind her fan, "*that* was much." And now it was she who wouldn't go away. She showered him with letters and invitations and requests for favors. He finally had to pretend he was out of town to get her to leave him alone. What a comical ending to the great love of his youth!

Over the years, Dickens had lived in many houses. As a child he had moved constantly, always deeper and deeper into poverty. Now his moves were always to better and larger houses as his family—and his income—increased. But on Friday, March 14, 1856, his wanderings ended when he bought the lovely old brick house on a hill that he had so admired as a boy. In a hopeful moment his own father had told him that he might someday live there—if he worked very hard. Dickens was to say that all the important events in his life had taken place on a Friday—his birth, his marriage, and the purchase of Gad's Hill Place, the house that symbolized the achievement of his childhood dreams.

With great joy he threw himself into improving the house. He hired painters and paperhangers to freshen the inside. He drilled a new well and had the slate roof raised so that extra rooms could be put in the attic. He bought cartloads of furniture under the pretense that his servant was buying them, so he could get a better price. "If you should meet such a thing as a mahogany dining table," he wrote, "in a donkey cart anywhere... you may be sure the property is mine."

For the fourteen years he lived there, Dickens never stopped adding little touches to the house. His study was on the ground floor at the front. He placed his desk before a large window so that he could enjoy the view and the light. The walls of the room were lined with bookshelves, and Dickens thought it would be fun to have the inside of the door disguised as a bookshelf, too, so that when he was inside with the door closed, he was surrounded by books. The fake books were all embossed in gold with fanciful titles, such as *Noah's Arkitecture* and *Cat's Lives* (in nine volumes, of course).

At last, Charles Dickens had more than a house. He had a home.

Some years before, the Dickens family had taken up temporary residence in Genoa, Italy, to save money. There he wrote his second Christmas book, *The Chimes*. He was so excited by the story that he traveled all the way back to London to read it to his friends before it was published.

On the night of December 3, 1844, a small group assembled at the home of John Forster to listen to *The Chimes*. Dickens read dramatically, imitating the voices and accents of the characters. It was an unforgettable performance. Rumors of the event were soon all over London.

From that time on, Dickens did more and more readings, sometimes for the public to raise money for charity. But any excuse would do. The attention, the excitement, the power to move his audience to grief or terror all thrilled him. It occurred to him that "a great deal of money might possibly be made" if he were to do readings for profit. Some of his friends thought the idea was beneath the dignity of a great author. But Dickens was responsible for an enormous family—not only his wife and children, but also his parents and his less successful brothers. He wanted to be sure that they would be provided for when he died.

MR. CHARLES DICKENS'S
READING.

Doors open at half past 7.
The Audience are respectfully requested to be in their places by 10 minutes to 8 o'clock.
ONE SHILLING.
The Reading will last two hours.

For the last fifteen years of his life, Dickens had two professions: author and actor. He was equally successful at both, for the combination of his wonderful words, stunning performances, and personal fame caused a sensation. The tickets sold out everywhere he went, and a great deal of money *was* made. Driven by the excitement and the profits, he traveled all over the country, working too hard and rarely resting. It was not surprising that his health began to fail.

Against the advice of his family and his doctor, Dickens agreed to return to the United States for a series of readings. It had been twenty-five years since he had been there and written so harshly about the Americans. He was older now and had seen more of the world. He conceded that perhaps he had wronged America a little. And the country had changed, too. Slavery had been abolished, and the rough frontier towns were becoming more civilized.

But one thing hadn't changed—the people were just as wild to see the famous Dickens as ever. They stood all night in the bitter cold to buy tickets to his readings, and the tour was a fabulous success. But it came at a high price. As his doctor had feared, Dickens became seriously ill. He was barely able to attend the farewell dinner given for him in New York. He arrived an hour late, and he could not walk without assistance. He gave a brief speech, then returned immediately to his room to lie down.

On the day he left, he was showered with flowers and cheers outside his hotel. As his ship pulled out, he waved his hat to the crowd on the dock and, with much warmth and the touch of a showman, he called to them—echoing Tiny Tim—"God bless you, every one!"

Once home, he allowed himself only a short rest before agreeing to a "farewell tour" of one hundred readings. His family was horrified, fearing it would kill him. But Charles Dickens was a stubborn man.

To make things worse, he added a new piece to his repertoire—the scene from *Oliver Twist* in which Nancy is murdered by Sikes. The piece was high drama, and it frequently caused ladies in the audience to faint. Dickens loved the scene so much that he performed it often. But it caused his blood pressure to soar, his face to turn red, and left him exhausted and ill afterward.

Finally, weakened by a stroke that affected his speech, he knew he had to stop. He had completed seventy-four of the hundred readings. On that last night, he stood before the audience with tears running down his cheeks and said, "From these garish lights, I now vanish forevermore, with a heartfelt, grateful, respectful, affectionate farewell." He kissed his hand to the crowd and limped off the stage.

He retired to Gad's Hill Place, hoping to recover his health. In the garden was a Swiss chalet, where he liked to write when the weather was nice. It had been a surprise gift from a friend, who had bought the little house in Switzerland and had it taken apart, packed into fifty-eight wooden crates, and sent to Dickens in England.

He was working there on a new novel, *The Mystery of Edwin Drood.* All his life he had liked to write in the morning and take long walks in the afternoon. But on June 8, 1870, he returned to the chalet after lunch and worked through the afternoon. He must have known that this was the novel he wouldn't finish, and he just wanted to write a little more.

That evening he suffered a massive stroke, and the following day he died, worn out, at only fifty-eight.

Many years have passed since Charles Dickens died, and the world is greatly changed. Yet the brilliance of his personality and the England he knew live on in the pages of his books. To read his stories is to be drawn into his special territory, where he becomes a beloved friend and guide. His quick mind and unexpected turn of phrase will catch you suddenly and make you laugh out loud. He will introduce you to his fascinating friends, and you will never forget them— not Uriah Heep or Betsy Trotwood or Ebineezer Scrooge or so many, many more.

Often he will invite you to walk with him through the streets of London. Staying clear of the horses and carriages, you will make your way carefully through the mud and filth into the darkest slums. He will show you the broken-down houses and the hollow-eyed, desperate people who live there. And among them will be a heartsick, lonely boy, shabby and hungry but still clinging to his dreams. Dickens will tighten his hold on your hand, and you will see that there are tears in his eyes.

When at last you put down the book, it will be regretfully, like saying good-bye to a friend after an exciting adventure together. But you will also know that you can go back again anytime you want, and he will be there, waiting.

BIBLIOGRAPHY

Ackroyd, Peter. *Dickens.* New York: HarperCollins, 1990.

Chesterton, G. K. *Charles Dickens.* New York: Schocken Books, 1965.

*Clarke, Penny. *Growing up During the Industrial Revolution.* London: B.T. Batsford, 1980.

Forster, John. *The Life of Charles Dickens.* New York: Doubleday, 1928.

*Haines, Charles. *Charles Dickens.* New York: Franklin Watts, 1969.

*Hunter, Nigel. *Charles Dickens.* New York: Bookwright, 1989.

Johnson, Edgar. *Charles Dickens: His Tragedy and Triumph.* 2 vols. New York: Simon and Schuster, 1952.

Kaplan, Fred. *Dickens: A Biography.* New York: Avon Books, 1990.

Priestley, J. B. *Charles Dickens: A Pictorial Biography.* New York: Viking, 1962.

Wilson, Angus. *The World of Charles Dickens.* New York: Viking, 1979.

Works by Charles Dickens used as sources for this biography:

American Notes: For General Circulation
Bleak House
The Chimes
A Christmas Carol: In Prose
Great Expectations
Hard Times
The Life and Adventures of Nicholas Nickleby
The Mystery of Edwin Drood
The Old Curiosity Shop
Oliver Twist; or, The Parish Boy's Progress
Our Mutual Friend
The Personal History of David Copperfield
The Posthumous Papers of the Pickwick Club
A Tale of Two Cities

*These books will be helpful to young readers interested in further research.